Table of Contents

I0487533

End User License Agreement

This book (the "Book") is a product provided by the ExamREVIEW PRESS (being referred to as "ExamREVIEW" in this document), subject to your compliance with the terms and conditions set forth below. PLEASE READ THIS DOCUMENT CAREFULLY BEFORE ACCESSING OR USING THE BOOK. BY ACCESSING OR USING THE BOOK, YOU AGREE TO BE BOUND BY THE TERMS AND CONDITIONS SET FORTH BELOW. IF YOU DO NOT WISH TO BE BOUND BY THESE TERMS AND CONDITIONS, YOU MAY NOT ACCESS OR USE THE BOOK. EXAMREVIEW MAY MODIFY THIS AGREEMENT AT ANY TIME, AND SUCH MODIFICATIONS SHALL BE EFFECTIVE IMMEDIATELY UPON POSTING OF THE MODIFIED AGREEMENT ON THE CORPORATE SITE OF EXAMREVIEW. YOU AGREE TO REVIEW THE AGREEMENT PERIODICALLY TO BE AWARE OF SUCH MODIFICATIONS AND YOUR CONTINUED ACCESS OR USE OF THE BOOK SHALL BE DEEMED YOUR CONCLUSIVE ACCEPTANCE OF THE MODIFIED AGREEMENT.

Restrictions on Alteration
You may not modify the Book or create any derivative work of the Book or its accompanying documentation. Derivative works include but are not limited to translations.

Restrictions on Copying
You may not copy any part of the Book unless formal written authorization is obtained from us.

LIMITATION OF LIABILITY
ExamREVIEW will not be held liable for any advice or suggestions given in this book. If the reader wants to follow a suggestion, it is at his or her own discretion. Suggestions are only offered to help.

IN NO EVENT WILL EXAMREVIEW BE LIABLE FOR (I) ANY INCIDENTAL,

CONSEQUENTIAL, OR INDIRECT DAMAGES (INCLUDING, BUT NOT LIMITED TO, DAMAGES FOR LOSS OF PROFITS, BUSINESS INTERRUPTION, LOSS OF PROGRAMS OR INFORMATION, AND THE LIKE) ARISING OUT OF THE USE OF OR INABILITY TO USE THE BOOK. EVEN IF EXAMREVIEW OR ITS AUTHORIZED REPRESENTATIVES HAVE BEEN ADVISED OF THE POSSIBILITY OF SUCH DAMAGES, OR (II) ANY CLAIM ATTRIBUTABLE TO ERRORS, OMISSIONS, OR OTHER INACCURACIES IN THE BOOK.

You agree to indemnify, defend and hold harmless ExamREVIEW, its officers, directors, employees, agents, licensors, suppliers and any third party information providers to the Book from and against all losses, expenses, damages and costs, including reasonable attorneys' fees, resulting from any violation of this Agreement (including negligent or wrongful conduct) by you or any other person using the Book.

Miscellaneous.

This Agreement shall all be governed and construed in accordance with the laws of Hong Kong applicable to agreements made and to be performed in Hong Kong. You agree that any legal action or proceeding between ExamREVIEW and you for any purpose concerning this Agreement or the parties' obligations hereunder shall be brought exclusively in a court of competent jurisdiction sitting in Hong Kong.

Say NO to fraud!

Why do you need to be so concerned about consumer committed fraud? Because consumer committed fraud is a major source of **risk** for small businesses doing business in the online world.

This book was written basing on real life experience fighting fraud.

We had invested into a small retail outfit selling outdoor hobby items on the internet. The target audiences were those teenagers and young hobbyists who are often less mature but clever enough to play dirty tricks through taking advantage of the loopholes along the payment process. Having to eat the losses from time to time, we made up our mind in changing the entire way of handling sales and payment and were then successfully cut down the defraud rate by almost 90%.

The goal of writing this book is to share our experience with you. We want to tell you how we have protected ourselves from consumer fraud, and how you can achieve the same. Instead of going highly technical, we wrote the book in such a way that it would be an easy-read for you, that you can use the techniques right away for your fraud prevention effort.

The Anti-Fraud Team
26 August, 2008

(i) "Risk is a concept that managers use to express their concerns about the probable effects of an uncertain environment. Because the future cannot be predicted with certainty, managers have to consider a range of possible events that could take place"[1]

As mentioned by David McNamee in his article "Management Control Concepts", uncertainty and randomness exist in nature and life, that risk is not something to be worried or concerned about but something to be managed. You just can't live without risk(s). Let's face it – fraud exists everywhere on the internet. In particular, consumer committed frauds pose a serious threat to the resource-limited small businesses. Even the most wary and sophisticated business managers may fall victim to consumer committed frauds. To survive, you need to learn how to manage such risk.

---

[1] http://www.mc2consulting.com/riskart2.htm.

(i) "Risk management is a discipline for dealing with uncertainty"[2].The processes of identifying, analyzing and assessing, mitigating, or transferring risk can be characterized as Risk Management. At the core of the Risk Management process we need to go through two primary stages. At the first stage, the following questions are to be answered:

? What could happen (the event) -> how could we be defrauded?

? If it happened, how bad could it be (the impact) -> what losses would we suffer when defrauded?

? How often could it happen (the frequency) -> how often would we be defrauded?

? How certain is it (uncertainty) -> are we likely be defrauded on a regular basis?

---

[2] http://www.nonprofitrisk.org/tutorials/rm_tutorial/2.htm.

Based on an in-depth understanding of the above issues, stage two deals with the following questions:

❓ What can be done for risk mitigation -> **how to fight fraud**?

❓ How much will it cost? -> **how much would it cost to fight fraud**?

❓ Is it cost effective -> **is it effective and affordable to fight fraud this way**?

This book deals with all the above issues in a clear and concise manner, with a razor sharp focus on consumer committed frauds. The ultimate goal is to help you set up a mechanism to proactively deter fraud – that is, to **stop it before it occurs**. In fact, **deterrence** is the key word agreed on by the anti-fraud professionals[3]. It is the most affordable way of fighting fraud.

---

[3] Refer to the article written by Mr. Dick Carozza on pg 25 of the Fraud Magazine (Vol 19 No. 5, 2005).

How could you be defrauded through the credit card system?

I am not trying to scare you here, but these are what can happen if you sell and deliver goods to a fraudster:

- Through a carrier you delivered a computer to a fraudster. The fraudster used the computer extensively for a month or so, then called his credit card company to file an "item not as described" dispute, accusing you of shipping a computer of inferior quality to him. The credit card company issued him a refund before he returns the computer to you.

- Through a carrier you delivered a computer to a fraudster. The fraudster took all the expensive parts out of the computer casing, then called his credit card company to file an "item damaged" dispute, accusing you of shipping a non-functioning computer to him. The credit card company issued him a refund before he returns the computer to you.

- Through a carrier you delivered a computer to a fraudster. He asked his friend to wait right in front of the doorway and impersonate him to sign for and collect the computer. Afterwards, he called up his credit card company to file an "item not received" dispute. The credit card company issued him a refund so he had both the money and the computer.

- Through a carrier you delivered a computer to a fraudster supplied address which is different from his actual billing address. He then called up his credit card company and claimed that he had never authorized such a purchase. The credit card company issued him a refund so he had both the money and the computer.

The above are just some examples of how fraudsters could defraud you through the credit card system.

Credit Card Chargeback

A chargeback occurs when a customer disputes a transaction and subsequently reverses the charge[4]. The entire chargeback process can be complicated and frustrating. First, the buyer contacts his credit

---

[4] The definition of chargeback is available at http://strategicwebventures.com/definitions/Glossary/Chargeback/. URL accessed and verified on Jan 4th of 2005.

card–issuing bank to initiate a refund for a purchase made on his card. The bank then researches the validity of the dispute and provides a provisional credit to him. Next, the bank initiates the process by obtaining credit from the credit card merchant account through the merchant's processing bank. The merchant's processing bank then performs their own research and validation. The merchant's bank either declines the chargeback and returns it to the card-issuing bank, or removes the chargeback amount from the credit card merchant account and provides written notification to the merchant.

When a notification is received, the merchant has to provide documentation to resolve the chargeback. If the documentation is satisfactory, the chargeback is declined and the customer is charged again for the sale. However, if the documentation is unsatisfactory, the chargeback is successful and the claim process is ended unless you choose to appeal further, which can be very costly and time consuming.

Filing chargeback request

> Generally speaking, a credit card user has 60 days from the statement date to file a chargeback request.

Cybershoplifting

As described by Wikipedia[5], chargebacks occur when a cardholder's credit card details are used to purchase items without their authorization. This generally involves online companies, who often cannot verify that the person entering the details on their site is the actual cardholder. When the cardholder becomes aware of the activity they usually notify their bank, who are likely to refund almost all of the costs. These costs are then passed back to the company involved as a "chargeback", effectively a penalty for accepting the transaction without proper verification of the purchaser's identity.

Another type of chargeback occurs when a legitimate

---

[5] http://en.wikipedia.org/wiki/Credit_card_fraud.

cardholder uses the card to purchase goods, or a service, and then when the statement comes, claims that they never authorized the transaction, or they never received goods or service ordered. This is also known as Cybershoplifting or first-party fraud.

Chargeback reason codes

Credit card companies have different reason codes for consumer chargeback[6], and it has been well known that decisions are most of the time in favor of the buyers due to the need for maintaining "customer satisfaction". In one internet forum there are many sellers who talk about their chargeback experiences[7]. As commented by one of the forum participants, in the case of a dispute the presumption is almost always in the customer's favor and that the terms of the merchant account agreement are often stacked against the sellers.

---

[6] Further information can be found at http://www.atlanticpayment.com/cardterms/chargeback.htm or through VISA's chargeback management guide VBS050102.

[7] The URL of the forum is http://www.webmasterworld.com/forum22/1044.htm.

Chargeback can mostly be established when a buyer claims that the good purchased was never delivered, when a buyer claims that the good received is not as described, or when a stolen credit card number was used for the purchase (meaning the purchase was unauthorized). In fact, many US banks provide chargeback dispute form that can be downloaded from the web[8].

AVS and CVV2

Both AVS and CVV2 are intended for fraud prevention (primarily against the stolen card claim).

AVS (Address Verification Service) refers to the technology that allows merchants to verify information regarding the credit card's billing address as supplied by the buyer. With AVS, when the card is processed, the merchant is informed whether or not the information matches that which is on file with the credit card

---

[8] The URL for downloading such form is http://www.utexas.edu/admin/purchasing/docs/pdf/dispute.pdf.

company, which gives merchants a chance to intervene prior to deciding to accept or deny a questionable order.

AVS alone is often not an adequate means of protection. Perceptive merchants also like to use the CVV2 codes for additional verification. These codes are typically presented as 3 digits on the reverse of a credit card that can be requested during a transaction. If the numbers fail to match, fraud may be present. The use of these codes can reduce credit card victimization considerably IF the thief doesn't have the card in his possession.

The card issuing bank will always ask the buyer to resolve the problem directly with you prior to doing a chargeback. However, it is fairly easy to say that you are "unreachable", that no one ever pick up the phone in your office, or that his emails to you often remain unanswered. In any case the bank is not going to verify these accusations, so that's why it is so easy for chargeback to be established.

Disputing Chargeback

Generally speaking, if you are using the payment service provided by your ecommerce service provider rather than to have your own merchant account, the service provider will handle the dispute process for you but most of the time you will lose (as the service provider would not want to spend too much resources on defending your interest):

Ecommerce service provider: send us all the info you have on the transaction.

You the seller: Here is the information you requested...

Ecommerce service provider: buyer says his credit card was used without his authorization. Bye.

You need to have a merchant account in order to dispute a chargeback. Your bank is not going to help you – you are totally on your own in defending yourself. Before going ahead, ask yourself this question: how many hours of work does it take in order to win a case, and how much money do you have afterwards, as compared to what you would have if you just left it?

As an advice ...

You need to strike a balance between using your time & resources wisely and defending what you know was a legitimate charge.

Remember, chargeback dispute can be extremely costly in terms of time and resources. Try to avoid them as much as you can.

Goods never delivered

Regarding the claim of "good never delivered", the

official requirement to defend is to provide proof that the good was received, such as any delivery receipt; signed invoice, customer name and delivery address ...etc[9]. As said before, not all delivery methods provide tracking functionality. Also, the buyer may simply ask someone else to sign for the delivery so that the signature on the delivery receipt does not match the signature on the buyer's credit card. **Many carriers simply would NOT verify signatures carefully.**

A major US retailer has something like this, which is defintiely NOT recommended when payment fraud is a concern:

"In most cases, by completing a delivery release form and leaving it where a driver can collect it, your order can be left at your home or office. If you have not completed this form, the driver may still leave your merchandise under some circumstances."

---

[9] Refer to http://www.e-bankcard.com/faqframe.htm.

Forged signature
By the way, signatures can be forged too...

Goods not as described

Regarding the claim of "good received not as described", the seller can submit product documentation and sales record as proof that the good was not mis-represented, but if the buyer said that what he/she had received was a box of stone or that the quality of the good is substantially inferior, then the seller is most likely out of luck. A variation of this claim is the saying of good received not functioning (i.e. defective or damaged). Again, it is very difficult to provide proof as no one really knows who had caused the defect or the damage.

Stolen card

Regarding the claim of "stolen card", the seller may provide proof that the shipping address is the same as the cardholder's credit card billing address, or that the cardholder's signature was presented. Since a cardholder's signature is very difficult (if not impossible) to be obtained on an internet transaction, the only way a seller can prevent this kind of chargeback is to ship to the buyer's card billing address. However, there are times when the buyers said the goods ordered were gifts for someone else, or that the goods need to be shipped to the office addresses as no one would be home to accept the delivery. Moreover, the credit card imprint and the cardholder's signature are the only proof accepted by Visa and MasterCard, electronic transactions can present a high risk of chargeback and that the recourse available to the sellers is minimal[10].

[10] Refer to http://www.busams.com/guide/chargeback.htm. URL accessed and verified on Jan 4th of 2005.

> Whenever a stolen card is involved, the customer (almost) always wins.

Why's the "not as described" claim invincible?

When such a claim is presented to the bank, the most you can do is to provide documentation which shows the corresponding product description & specifications and possibly some pictures of the product shipped. The buyer may do the same by taking pictures of what he had received. Since there is no one on his site to monitor the process, he may simply take pictures of a bunch of rocks and claim that these are what you have sent him. When disagreement of this sort arises, the buyer is often the one to be trusted UNLESS he has made similar claims too often in the past.

For a defective item claim to be honored, the buyer's bank will instruct the buyer to first return the defective item back to you. As soon as he has the proof of shipment handy (all he needs is proof of shipment, NOT proof of successful delivery) the entire amount will be credited back to his account. The bank doesn't really care if you actually receive the returned item or if a box of trash is what has been sent back to you.

Why would the credit card companies rule in

favor of the consumers most of the time?

It is widely believed that a lot of the time chargeback is just a legitimate form of credit card fraud. In fact, based on a study by the Gartner Group, about 1.1% of online transactions are estimated to result in fraudulent chargeback committed by buyers[11].

The topic of consumer rights protection has been around for decades. John F. Kennedy who was the president of America in 1962 once in his speech expressed four basic consumer rights, which are the Right to Safety, the Right to Choose, the Right to Information and the Right to be Heard (Barksdale

---

[11] The Paypal official estimate is available at http://www.paypal.com/cgi-bin/webscr?cmd=p/sell/chargeback_risk-outside. URL accessed and verified on Jan 4th of 2005.

and French, 1976). Consumer protection, therefore, refers to protection of these rights, and covers the wide range of topics that includes and not limited to product liability, fraud and misrepresentation (Wikipedia, 2004).

Although we have not seen any widely held consensus on the justification for consumer protection, from a legal perspective, as described by Overby (2001), we can come up with the following general aims:

- to create efficient markets for goods and services
- to advance ethical goals
- to paternalise the protection of the consumer

As said by Vogel, the stringency and scope of consumer protection have expanded significantly across all industrialized countries since 1960s (2002). In the US for example, an era of progressive activism in the 60s and the 70s had prompted a wave of legislation geared towards the advancement of consumer rights, which eventually made consumer protection a major function of the US government and its 50 federal agencies (Steiner and Steiner 2002, pg 542-543).

While traditional consumer protection measures were designed for the brick and mortar environment, the same principles can be applied towards the internet. As described by Andrews and Shen (2000), there is increasing attention given to consumer protection in the virtual world because people will step back if they believe that they are more vulnerable to abuses online.

Along with the rise in the level of consumer protection, at the same time we are seeing demand for quality at a level way beyond the traditional implied warranty of merchantability and warranty of fitness for a particular purpose[12]. The heightened emphasis on consumer protection coupled with increased regulations is believed to frequently put legitimate and honest businesses into troubles (Hooker, 2002).

---

[12] The legal definition of warranties can be found at http://www.lectlaw.com/files/cos53.htm. URL accessed and verified on Jan 2nd of 2005.

Satisfaction Guarantee

The importance of consumer satisfaction in buyer behavior is well recognized, as it is widely agreed that it is an element critical to the success of a business in the long run (Rust, Zahorik, and Keiningham, 1995).

Satisfaction guarantee originated from the rationale that when buying remotely, at the time of the purchase the product quality is highly uncertain to the consumer (Wernerfelt, 1994). It is not the same as manufacturer warranty. With manufacturer warranty, the manufacturer provides replacement, refund or repair works only if the product is defective within the warranty period under normal use (Heal, 1977). Satisfaction guarantee, on the other hand, is provided by the seller, often in the form of "no questions asked guarantee" (Davis, Gerstner and Hagerty, 1995).

Different interpretations can be applied to the term "Guarantee" in different contexts, but generally speaking such a guarantee represents a promise (Callan and Moore, 1998) which aims at making the customer happy (Evans, Clark, and Knutson, 1996) through explaining to the customer what product or service can be expected and how he/she will be compensated if the product or service is not as expected when delivered (Hart, Schlesinger, and Maher, 1992). Some companies even believe that customer should be satisfied regardless of whatever cost it takes, that it is the customer's privilege to take advantage of the business several times a year (see Lund, 2000).

Even though previous studies suggest that promises made to the customers in the form of guarantee can cause firms to improve their product or service delivery processes (Wirtz 1998; Priest 1981), in today's highly competitive world most businesses are already well aware of the need for quality that they do have substantial incentives to produce and provide quality products (Manley II and Shrode, 1990). The problem is, what seems to be of high quality in the eyes of the producer may not translate to high customer perceived quality. And more importantly, satisfaction guarantee can be very costly to implement. As Schmidt and Kernan (1985) said, a satisfaction guarantee policy may make certain products unprofitable for the sellers even though certain manufacturers and distributors may be willing to take back the returned products for a partial or full refund (Padmanabhan and Png, 1997).

While it was argued that satisfaction guarantee can stimulate sales by reducing the risks of the consumers and increasing their willingness to buy (Davis, Gerstner and Hagerty, 1995), return policies that are too liberal may encourage further returns by free-riders (Lutz 1989). Even if the buyers are honest, product returns still incur extra cost on the part of the sellers in the form of lost sales and handling of salvaged products. In the context of the internet, product returns become even more expensive due to the need to ship back and forth the products in question. As said by Moorthy and Srinivasan (1995), using satisfaction guarantee to signal high product quality is viable only if the seller's transaction cost is low.

Customer perceived quality and expectation

When talking about quality we often come across the issue of expectations. Unlike problems such as non-delivery or defective on arrival which usually have a clear-cut yes and no answer, quality is often a subjective matter. As described by Northcutt (1997), quality is an element which is "in the eye of the beholder", therefore the degree of expectation which determines the perceived quality can vary among consumers, as one's perception on a product really deals with the psychological processing of the product information as received by the senses of that individual (Mullen and Johnson, 1990). It is possible that some consumers are having unreasonable expectations, or that expectations are being used as an excuse for returning the unwanted products. There has been study showing that some consumers did have expected product performance well beyond the realistic limit under documented reasonable usage (see Loe, Ferrell, and Mansfield, 2000). And regardless of the impact on cost structure brought by the need for providing guarantees, satisfaction guarantee seems to have become something most modern consumers are expecting:

(i) *"Consumers of products and now services are coming to expect a 100% satisfaction guarantee whether it's for a Hershey chocolate bar or for H&R Block tax preparation services." (Lee, 2001)*

Although we cannot rule out the possibilities of merchants cheating consumer through offering goods of inferior quality, it is also not uncommon to find consumers who are totally unreasonable and are demanding for unrealistic guarantee based on illogical rationales. For example, Elbert Wade, a Professional Certified Consultant Astrologer had once encountered a customer who asked him to guarantee that what he says about the future will come true[13].

Paypal in the equation

Paypal can't stop chargeback. Regardless of whatever being said in the Paypal User Agreement, there is just no way for it to stop chargeback (because consumer rights almost always override anything else). It may fight chargeback in some cases, but it has totally no way to stop its users from filing chargeback requests with the banks. And there is no guarantee that Paypal will win every chargeback case. So what this means is that, at the

---

[13] The URL of this story is http://www.elbertwade.com/page63.html. URL accessed and verified on Jan 2nd of 2005.

end of the day, either Paypal itself or the merchant will have to "eat the loss".

So why would Paypal make things even riskier for sellers? In a pure credit card scenario, the fraudster's only option is to file chargeback with his bank and nothing else. With Paypal, he can first make claim against you through Paypal's own facility without getting his bank involved. If Paypal rejects his claim, he can then take the matter to his bank and override Paypal's decision. Paypal is effectively giving him one extra option for abusing you!

Frozen Paypal account

Paypal can't really find out what had actually happened between you and the buyer. When a chargeback occurs, Paypal may freeze BOTH accounts.

The rationale is simple – Paypal doesn't know you. It doesn't know your buyer as well. When a chargeback takes place, the money is withdrawn from the Paypal system to an outsider (the credit card bank and subsequently the buyer's pocket). Therefore, it is technically possible for the seller to work with the buyer to intentionally defraud Paypal. This is why Paypal will freeze BOTH accounts, then asks you to fax in a bunch of documents to prove that you guys are really doing serious business but not running a scam, and take time to perform such investigation.

Paypal may even ask you to provide information originated from your product supplier, such as invoices and payment receipts. If you are using Paypal as your primary payment processor, be sure to have ALL paperworks from your supplier handy all the time. If you are selling your own creation, invoices for the build material should do the job.

The whole process can take months to complete, and you may ultimately lose your money if the money cannot be recovered from the fraudster's account. In some cases a collection agent may come into play since the balance you owe Paypal is technically a debt:

"We appreciate your interest in PayPal. Unfortunately our decision to close your account is final.

PayPal reserves the right to close any account reported to be involved in possible fraudulent or high risk behavior. In the event of a dispute, PayPal will seek to recover the funds from you by debiting your PayPal balance and, if there are not sufficient funds in your PayPal balance, PayPal reserves the right to collect your debt to PayPal by any other legal means."

To ship or not to ship with a frozen account

You would still have to ship even when your $ is frozen. Since the receiver of the transaction is PayPal, Paypal is technically the MERCHANT OF RECORD (the merchant of record typically has to take responsibility for all payment charge backs and fraud) from a payment perspective. However, Paypal has made it clear upfront that it is only a payment service provider, that it has nothing to do with the goods provided by the seller. In other words, it does not participate in the business activities between the seller and the buyer.

As an advice ...

When you sign up to use Paypal you are assumed to have gone through the Terms of Use. You are basically bound to agree with the role of Paypal being strictly a payment processing service provider and nothing else.

As a seller, you have a contractual duty to deliver the ordered goods to the buyer. On the other hand, the buyer has the contractual duty to pay. If the buyer pays and then reverses the charge, he breaks the contract. If he lies by claiming unauthorized purchase, he commits a crime. But if he pays in full per your request, then he has done his part of the deal and it is now your turn to do your part.

If you choose to receive payment through Paypal, then you must deliver when the money reaches your Paypal account. It does not matter whether the money would actually go into your pocket.

The key here is that the buyer has made payment basing on your instructions (and that the Paypal account is in your name). Regardless of how the money is withheld by Paypal or by any other middlemen, you as the seller must fulfill your obligation by delivering the ordered goods, or the buyer can sue you for breach of contract.

After shipment is made, you may focus on resolving the dispute with Paypal. Remember, Paypal is to provide a service to the seller to receive electronic transactions on the sellers behalf and then pass those proceedings to the seller for a service fee. PayPal has, in theory, breached the contract by failing to perform this function. The point is, this is strictly a business problem between you the seller and Paypal. The buyer has no role in this contractual relationship at all.

If you really don't want to ship in the case of a frozen account, take the following steps to make sure you don't get into legal troubles with the buyer:

- With all the evidences of frozen account you

have, inform the buyer BOTH verbally and in writing that this sudden tragedy has made it impossible for you to fulfill your obligation. It is NOT that you don't want to ship but is just that without the money you cannot afford to ship. Emphasis this to show that you have no criminal intention to defraud anyone at all. Put this in writing as well.

- Kindly request the buyer to file an item not received claim with Paypal. Paypal would have to give him back his money.

- With the buyer out of the equation, you can focus your effort on dealing with Paypal. You cannot get pass Paypal to work with the merchant bank directly anyway...

➡ **As an advice ...**
Using a friend or anyone else's name, address, personal info and bank cards to register a second account with Paypal is considered as Identify Theft. You could put them at risk of being charged with

> fraud as well.

Our recommendation to those who use Paypal for payment processing is that: use Paypal only for small and inexpensive items. If you are to sell expensive items, use a formal merchant account, OR accept other forms of payment, such as bank-to-bank transfer. Keep this in mind: Paypal was intended for processing micro-payments when it was first started.

Another common type of consumer committed fraud is check fraud.

"According to Rutgers University, a typical day in the United States results in almost two million checks written that will end up returned without payment or "bouncing". In a given year, about 500 million checks are forged"[14].

Technological advances have made it easier to duplicate and forge checks. Armed with a checking account number and a bank routing number (in the US, a routing transit number is a 9 digit number commonly found in the bottom part of a bank check), fraudsters can easily create checks almost on the fly. For example, at Qchex.com users can sign up to print checks through providing a working e-mail

---

[14] http://www.georgiaretail.org/CheckFraud.htm.

address alone and nothing else. There is almost no other attempt to verify their true identity[15]. On the other hand, it is believed that banks are automated to the point where bad checks can go through the system without ever being seriously examined[16].

Handling foreign checks

Foreign checks are even harder to verify. In any case, you may get yourself in deep trouble if you ship an item before the check is fully cleared in the banking system. A bad check will get noticed sooner or later, and the bank will go after you because you are the one who deposited the check, even though you have done so with full honest intent. **If the bad check is a foreign check, the chance of recovery is minimal.**

I don't mean to discriminate here, but certain countries are just too risky to deal with payment-wise. Pakistan, Nigeria, Malaysia, and Indonesia are among the worst.

---

[15] http://www.msnbc.msn.com/id/7914159.

[16] http://www.msnbc.msn.com/id/7914159/page/2/.

According to Legal-Definitions.com, fraud is defined "as a deception deliberately practiced to secure unfair or unlawful gain"[17], which could be a serious crime in some states (for example, fraud in Arizona is classified as class 2 felony and is defined by statute as "any person who, pursuant to a scheme or artifice to defraud, knowingly obtains any benefit by means of false or fraudulent pretenses, representations, promises or material omissions"). The words "deliberately" or "knowingly" spelled out the importance of the intention involved regardless of exactly what have been done to implement the fraud.

Fraud VS Scam

Another word which is often used interchangeably with fraud by the online communities is "scam", which means a dishonest scheme for making money[18]. Strictly speaking, "scam" and "fraud" do

---

[17] Refer to http://www.Legal-Definitions.com/fraud.htm.

[18] Refer to http://www.performanceprobe.com/extras/ebayscam.htm.

not share exactly the same definition. However, from a victim's point of view, between the two the difference is not significant, as long as the one who makes money out of it has been dishonest intentionally.

The element of fraudulent intent

The thing is, it is never easy for a merchant to prove one's fraudulent intent, especially with the presence of a legitimate channel (such as the chargeback mechanism). And it is never the job of an honest merchant like you to investigate and execute criminal. Strictly speaking, there are ways to get them arrested, especially when they have done the same thing a couple of times (such that the police have to get serious about it). However, the whole process can be extremely time and resource consuming, and you definitely would not want to get into this.

Sending a criminal behind bars is a complicated and expensive matter totally beyond your control. All that you should want to do is to make yourself a difficult target in the eyes of the fraudsters.

What is the UCC all about?

The common definition of online fraud seems to resemble part of the Uniform Commercial Code (UCC) defined Mail Fraud, which makes it a criminal offense for anyone to defraud through the use of the United States Postal Service (USPS)[19]. However, Mail Fraud demands a solid proof of defrauding intention and covers only mail order fraud schemes that leverage the USPS network, which may not be applicable if USPS is not involved in the transaction.

Many foreign countries have similar legislations in place. The exact details, however, often vary greatly.

---

[19] Refer to http://www.lectlaw.com/def2/m001.htm.

When you get defrauded, monetary loss is unavoidable. Apart from this, your entire business may also be unexpectedly affected. Let's think about this, what could be a major disaster to your online business?

The ability to accept payment!

Merchant account getting shuttered down ...

You run into a major disaster if your merchant account is shut down such that you could no longer accept credit card payment. This is a crucial issue that can affect your ability to continue running your business.

iii Repeated chargeback incidents can lead to account closure.

Below shows the chargeback policy of a major online credit card payment processor:

"Merchants that generate chargebacks cost us money and harm our reputation. From the merchant's account we deduct $15 per credit card chargeback. We will deduct an additional $35 penalty per credit card chargeback if the merchant's products generate in excess of 0.75% chargebacks in any 90 day period. **We reserve the right to close the merchant's account if excessive chargebacks occur.***"*

What is Business Continuity?

Account closure directly affects your ability to do business with your customers. In other words, business continuity is at risk.

Business continuity is a term that describes the processes and procedures an organization puts in place to ensure that essential functions can continue during and after a disaster. Business continuity planning (BCP) seeks to prevent interruption of mission-critical services, and to reestablish full functioning as swiftly and smoothly as possible. The very first step in business continuity planning is deciding which of the organization's functions are essential, and apportioning the available efforts / resources accordingly.

For most online businesses, credit card payment acceptance is the single most important function!

Getting a closed account back to work could be highly uneasy ☹

As part of any continuity planning effort, we often undertake what we called Business Impact Analysis (BIA), which involves identifying the critical business functions within the organization and determining the impact of NOT performing those functions beyond the maximum acceptable outage. Simply put, BIA leads you to think clearly about this question – For how long can your business survive without accepting credit card payment?

For your information...

A well done BIA should be capable of identifying costs linked to failures, such as loss of cash flow, loss of profits ...etc.

Now let's say you are not getting close to having a merchant account closure problem yet. What would be the loss in a single fraud incident?

✓ First you have the cost of the item. Remember, even if you manage to recover the item, the item is very likely to be in less than satisfactory condition – it may just be in a condition no longer suitable for resale.

✓ Next you have the S/H (shipping & handling) costs. In some circumstance you may actually have to pay S/H both ways when trying to recover the item. S/H can be expensive for large and heavy items.

✓ Bank fees – when you charge someone's card you pay a bank fee. When the charge is reversed you also pay a bank fee. Bank fees both ways can account for 5% of the transaction amount.

✓ Finally you have the opportunity cost – you lose another business opportunity by entertaining this fraudster in the first place.

Even if credit card payment has not been relied upon on by your business, check fraud and other payment frauds can still result in your suffering from monetary loss as well as loss of productivity and morale. Believe me, you will get very depressed, and may even lose your faith on your internet venture.

For your information...

Fighting chargeback is a time consuming process. It often takes a month or two for an initial ruling to be made by the bank, and it can take several more months if the customer chooses to appeal further.

How often could it happen, and how certain is it?

To answer these questions, you need to have a clear definition of your business. That is, you need to know what you are selling (price and product nature), and who are your target audiences. Let's first classify goods based on price. Such a classification can be industry-specific, and the price ranges shown below are for illustrative purpose only:

less risky

more risky

- dirt cheap item has a value below US$10
- low price item has a value between US$10 and US$50
- mid price item has a value between US$51 and US$100
- high price item has a value between US$101 and US$200
- deluxe item has a value between US$201 and US$500
- big ticket item has a value over US$500

Judging from price alone, the more expensive an item is, the more risk it carries as you can safely assume that a $10 item doesn't really worth a fraudster's effort. The exact "risky price range" for a specific product really depends on its nature, which dictates its customer base.

➥ **As an advice ...**

If you sell both high price items and low price items, you may want to differentiate your fraud prevention strategies accordingly. As long as you make your sales policy clear and straight forward, there shouldn't be much confusion introduced.

Talking about the nature of a product, it is best to illustrate through some real life examples. Let's say you are selling airsoft, a type of paintball like air gun replica which is extremely popular among teenagers. The customer base usually comprises school kids and young adults who do not necessarily have strong education background and stable incomes. On the other hand, if you are selling study guides for the AICPA exam (a professional exam for the accountants), you have a customer base primarily of educated and mature adults who are likely to have higher ethical standards (as ethics is one required element for getting professionally certified). So, airsoft VS study guides. Which customer group do you think would be more likely to give you trouble?

Profit and loss

Now you should have an idea on the overall level of risk your business is facing. If you are selling higher price items to a more troublesome group of customers, you face a higher risk. On the other hand, if you are selling to a nice group of customers, your overall risk is much lower.

Still, there is on more issue that has to be addressed. Ask yourself this question: if I got totally defrauded in one transaction (meaning you can hardly recover anything), how many more transactions would I have to make in order to compensate for the loss?

This is all about profit margin. If you have a fat margin (something like 30% or so), you can probably afford to be less skeptical because you may still easily recover through selling more. However, if your margin is thin (something like 10% or less), you may want to be very serious about the whole fraud issue as it would cost you quite a lot in order to catch up.

Calculating your loss expectancy

With the information you have on hand, it is time to combine the estimates for the value of potential loss and the probability of loss to develop an estimate of annual loss expectancy (ALE), which is useful for establishing your maximum acceptable risk in financial terms. For example, "do not accept more than a 1 in 100 chance of losing $100 in 2006" or "do not accept an ALE greater than $10,000 in 2007". The formula to use for such calculation is pretty simple:

Single Loss Expectancy (how bad each time)	x	Annualized Rate of Occurrence (how often would it happen)	=	Annualized Loss Expectancy

To make it simple without getting too technical: if every fraud incident can cost you $100, and about 10 such frauds are expected to occur this year, your simplified ALE is $1000. If you just started your business, it would be a little bit difficult to come up with an estimate of the rate of occurrence. This rate is determined mostly based on past experience or competitive information (the rate of your closest competitor).

→ As an advice ...

If you sell both high risk items and low risk items, always calculate their loss expectancies separately. For the best possible fraud prevention effect, you want to handle these items differently.

How could such risk be mitigated?

Now that you have got a clear idea on what can go wrong, the next thing that you should do is to make your decision on whether or not to take action to stop fraud before it hits you. You should base your decision on your ALE. If you are comfortable with your ALE, you may want to just sit back and do nothing. If, however, you think the ALE is too much for you, then you better be serious on finding ways to mitigate your risk.

Below are the key concerns on risk mitigation:

✔ What can be done for risk mitigation -> **how to fight fraud**?

✔ How much will it cost? -> **how much would it cost to fight fraud**?

✔ Is it cost effective -> **is it effective to fight fraud this way**?

Based on our experience, most credit card chargeback frauds involve the "unauthorized payment" claim and/or the "Stolen card" claim. Bad checks or forged checks could also be a threat but they might be less likely to occur as check fraud that exceeds a certain monetary sum is an outright felony in many states.

The key to mitigate payment fraud risk is to know your customers. You know their background, then you should be able to tell their intention. Think about it, would a person who lives in a $300-a-month apartment be capable of paying for a $6000 high tech gizmo? Probably not.

So how are you going to "background" check him? First of all, always insist on shipping to his credit card billing address. Then, with the address he provides, you can use one of the following free services to do some basic address and phone number verifications:

http://www.publicrecordfinder.com/peoplefind.html

Home | Submit A Link | Contact Us

▶ Free People Finder

Public Records Search			
First Name	**MI**	**Last Name**	**State**
			Nationwide ▾

☐ I entered a partial first name above   ✓ *Search*

→ Background Check   → Search By Social Security Number   → Search By Phone

http://www.anywho.com/

AnyWho online directory — AT&T   WE KNOW HOTELS INSIDE AND OUT.®   Find Deals in your Favorite Cities! New York ▾ GO!   hotels.com   **Internet Services** from AT&T

Finding People, Places, and Businesses

HOME   YELLOW PAGES   WHITE PAGES   REVERSE LOOKUP   HELP

> International
> Maps
> Area Codes
> Toll-Free

> Credit Center
> Shopping.com
> eHarmony.com
> eDiets.com
> Video News

LowerMyBills

FIND A BUSINESS

Business Category or Name *Required*

⊙ Category   ○ Name

City   State
            Select ▾   ⊙ SEARCH

FIND A PERSON

Last Name *Required*   First Name

TIP: Try just the 1st 4 letters   TIP: Use the 1st letter

City   State   Zip
            Select ▾   ⊙ SEARCH   → Search Tips

http://people.yahoo.com/

YAHOO! PEOPLE SEARCH Sign In
New User? Sign Up

Create / Edit My Listing - Remove My Listing

Try our free white pages search to access updated phone and address information.
Find friends, colleagues, classmates and more!

US Phone and Address Search
(Canada Phone and Address Search)

First Name/Initial: Last Name: (required)

City/Town: State:
                                   Entire USA

[Phone and Address Search]

Email Search

First Name/Initial: Last Name:

[Email Search]

These services allow you to legally search for a person or a business based on the name and location information you have on hand. The results they return (address and phone number) are usually quite accurate as they have access to the most updated public utility records of the search targets.

As an advice ...

The most basic pieces of information needed for doing an initial search are the person's first name, last name and state. For a more effective search, you will need to also supply the person's city and zip code.

For your information...

Similar search services are relatively rare in most foreign countries. Local phone companies often publish their yellow page directories on the WWW, but the search options are rather limited.

Also note that in some EU countries performing this kind of search may violate their data privacy law.

On the other hand, there are advanced fraud prevention services in the market which, for a fee, can perform address verification quite effectively. For example, each credit card has a bank identification number (BIN), which is the first six digits of the cc # which will always be the same. Some advanced fraud prevention facilities can verify a buyer's card BIN against his household address. If, let's say, a BIN indicates that a card was issued by a bank in New York but the customer is residing in California, fraud alert may be raised.

What to do if there is a match

If the address information returned matches the address supplied by the customer, you are generally safe with regards to payment authorization. Still, as mentioned before, you want to know the intent of the purchase. To make an educated estimate of the intent you want to know whether he can afford the purchase. Let's say your search target lives in Rocky Water Lane of San Jose, what you may want to do is to use a search engine (such as Yahoo or Google) to run search with the following search term: "real estate" "rocky water lane" "san jose". A number of real estate links will be returned, and you can click into one of them to find out more on the real estate prices in Rocky Water Lane and in the surrounding areas. You may even see pictures of houses around there. Based on the market value (for sale prices or rental fees) of houses around there, you can tell whether the purchaser is rich enough or not for the purchase.

For your information...

Search service like https://find.intelius.com/property-check.html also provides a property check service which, for a fee, gives you an in-depth report on information like Home Value, Ownership Info, Neighborhood Report, and Avg. Area Income, which may all be useful for assessing the financial status of the purchaser.

What to do if there is NO match found

If the addresses returned do not give a match, raise an alert but don't panic yet. Try a search through:

http://find.intelius.com/

- you enter your customer's information and retrieve his name and his confirmed current address. Since everyone of the phone numbers and addresses listed are verified against public utility, the results are reasonably accurate.

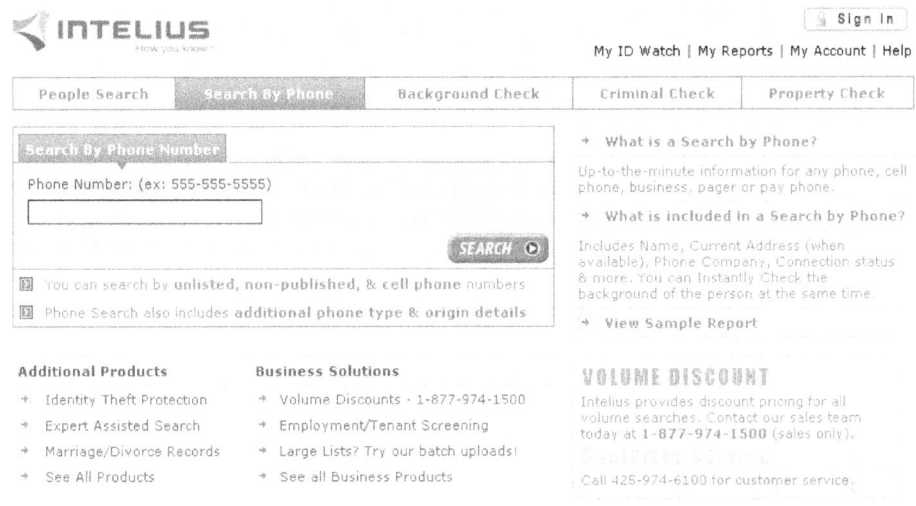

The service will cost you a fee, but you may find it worthwhile to spend this money if the transaction is a large one and you want to be sure you are not dealing with a fraudster.

We are not affiliated with this service. This service is recommended simply because we use it ourselves and we think it is great.

To quickly illustrate how easy it is to do a search, I type in the name and state of my customer then click on the Search button:

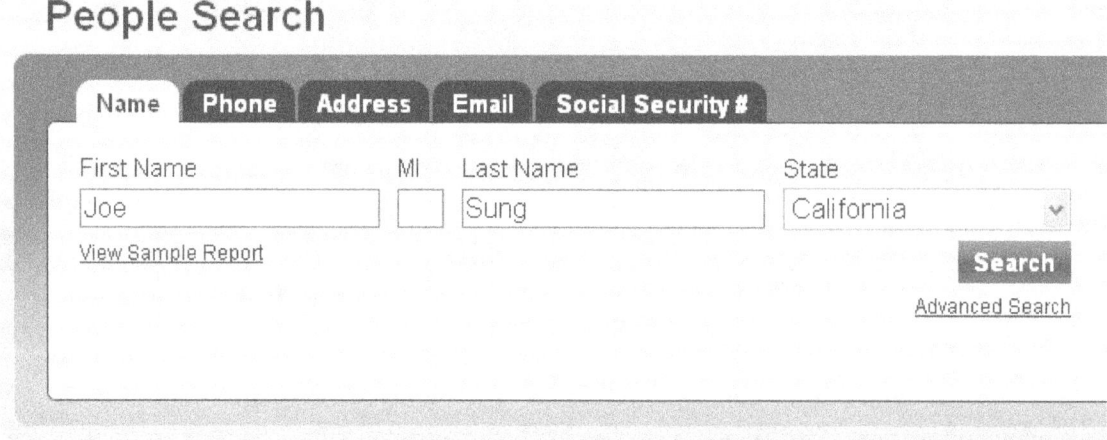

After about 2 seconds a result set with 8 matches

were listed:

<< Return to Home

PEOPLE SEARCH RESULTS

8 People found that match Joe Sung in the state of California.

Click on the Name or View Details link for more info.

✔ = Available Information

	NAME	AGE	PREVIOUS CITIES	DOB	PHONE	ADDRESS	AVG. INCOME	AVG. HOME VALUE	RELATIVES
1	Joef Sung View Details	55	San Jose, CA Milpitas, CA Sunnyvale, CA	✔	✔	✔	✔	✔	Joseph C Sung Staphnie Sung Joef Sung
2	Joe T P Sung View Details	65	San Leandro, CA San Francisco, CA Hayward, CA	✔	✔	✔	✔	✔	Tsai L Sung Ruth C Sung Irene A Sung Juliet C Sung Yen Ling Sung Scott Ty Sung Hui Mei Sung Wei L Sung Hui mei K Sung Yeiling Sung
3	Joe Sung View Details	45	Yorba Linda, CA Baldwin Park, CA Stanton, CA Long Beach, CA	✔	✔	✔	✔	✔	Joon H Sung Min Hyang Sung Bok H Sung
4	Joe T Sung View Details	65	San Ramon, CA	✔	✔	✔	✔	✔	Juliet C Sung Eric L Sung Chialing L Sung
	Joe Sung								

See Details on All 8 People!

I may then check them out one by one. The Average Income and Average Home Value columns are particularly useful – it gives you an idea whether the customer has the financial power to afford the purchase of an expensive item.

If you have the customer's phone number, a phone search (they call it Reverse Phone Lookup) can often produce more accurate results. Just type in the phone number:

and an exact match can be obtained:

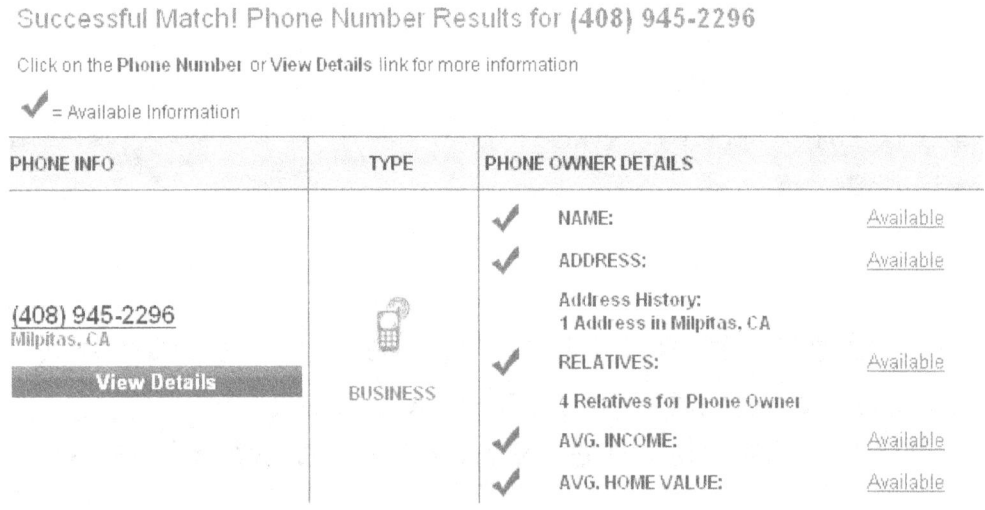

If the address information returned by these search services does not match the address information provided by the customer, you may want to request for further documentation from him and see how he responds. You want to do this through calling him and talking to him over the phone.

For your information...

Sometimes a fraudster will submit the actual phone number of the person whose card was stolen. A simple phone call in this case can reveal the fraud. In fact, if you are told that his phone number has been disconnected or the number has been changed, you may assume that the order is a fraudulent one.

If along the process of phone communication he insists on calling via his cell phone number, you must think twice before proceeding any further. Fraudsters like to make and receive calls via cell phones as these calls are much harder to trace and keep track of. On the other hand, a regular phone number is usually tied to a person registered with the local phone company, which makes it possible for law enforcement to track things down.

➥ As an advice...

To save time and efforts you may request your customer to fax in a copy of his latest utility bill for verification. However, utility bills can be forged as well, so you may not want to rely on it as your sole anti-fraud measure.

Some merchants actually require their customers to fax over their picture IDs for identity verification. While this used to be an effective measure in the past, advances in digital photography related technologies have made it easier to

---

create forged picture ID. And people in general dislike faxing over their IDs due to the fear of identity theft. This is why, at the end of the day, you will still need to do a bit of your own research. Requesting for a faxed copy of one's ID may be a sufficient measure for mid-price items (under the assumption that it doesn't worth a fraudster's time to go through the hassles) but may not be good enough when a high price item is involved.

Say "No" when necessary

Sometimes you may hear your customers saying something like:

"I am not home to receive the package. Please ship to my office instead."

"My girl friend is going to pay for this so please ship to her address."

"I am in the process of moving to a new home and I don't have the time to update my address information with the utility companies yet. Could you ship the item to my new address for now?"

If you want to avoid potential troubles, politely refuse and tell them that you are required to ship to the billing addresses and no where else. NEVER ship to any address other than the billing address on file or you risk taking chargeback.

Shipping to a different address

If your customer insists on shipping to another address and you don't want to lose his business, kindly offer to ship to his office. Ask him to fax you his business card, then do a free business search through:

http://www.anywho.com/

to ensure that this business is a legitimate one that really exists.

From the menu under the heading "Find a business", type in the business name and the location. Having the zip code handy would be most useful, but the city name would also do just fine.

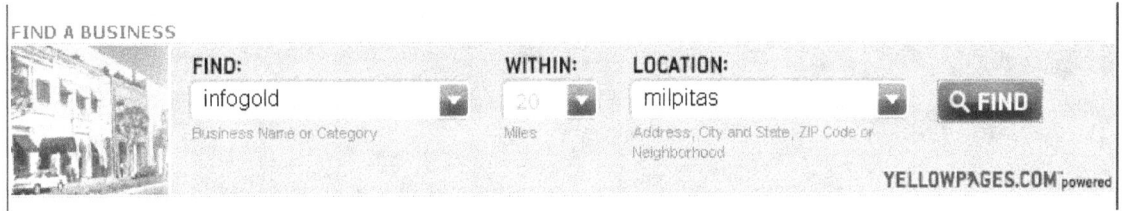

To go one step further, call the number returned by the search service and find out if your customer is really a current employee over there.

➡ **As an advice...**

Before making the shipment, ask this customer to sign and fax back a written authorization letter which authorizes you to ship to his specified alternate location. This may not stop the fraud, but having such a signed letter could make it much easier to prove his criminal intent.

If what you are selling is an extremely high price niche item (talking about several thousand dollars here) with a fat profit margin, you may want to invest a little bit more money on an in-depth background check against a potential new buyer. The search services previously mentioned include special paid packages for further background checking. There are also search services which specialize in criminal record checking, such as:

http://www.instantpeoplecheck.com

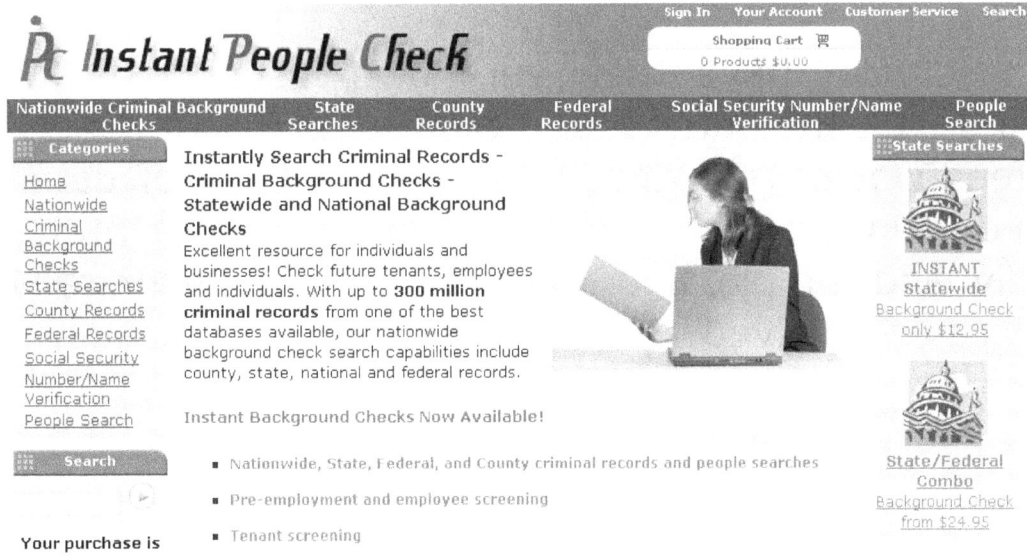

http://www.casebreakers.com/

Case Breakers
Global Intelligence Search Specialists .com

Free To Sign Up - No Monthly Fee - Pay As You Go!

Home | Sign Up | About Us | Contact Us | Press Release | Affiliate Program | Login Here

Locate People

Search by Name
Search by Social Security Number
Reverse Address Search
Reverse Phone Number Search
Phone Number Intelligence Pro

Background Checks

Personal Profile Report
Due Diligence Profile Report
Eviction Search
Bankruptcy, Liens & Judgments
Childcare Screening

Employment Screening

Social Security Number Verification
Education Verification
Employment Verification
Worker Compensation Claims
Professional License Verification

Criminal Records

County Criminal Search
State Criminal Search
Federal Criminal Search
National Criminal Index Search
State Criminal Index Search
Sex Offender Search

More Searches

Business Profile Report
Business Credit Report
Property Deed Search
Florida Accident Search
Motor Vehicle Driving History
Locate Lost Money

Fingerprinting & DNA Kit

These Child ID Kits provides the most comprehensive record of a child's identifying characteristics available today.
More Info

These services have their very own instructions for carrying out the intended search and investigation, and fees would vary depending on the level of detail desired. Don't worry, their interfaces are pretty friendly and simple and there is nothing technically complicated involved.

When a big ticket item is involved, you may want to, (for a small fee) obtain a credit report of the buyer. Site like http://www.accuratecredit.com/ provides credit reports with scores (usually under the Personal Credit Reports section) for less than $20 so you may judge whether the buyer is a high risk one (remember, fraudsters often have loads of bad debts piled up against them).

| Credit Reports | Criminal Records | Public Records | Driving Records | Free Applications |

Accurate

CREDIT BUREAU

IMPORTANT DECISIONS DEMAND ACCURATE INFORMATION
Phone 626 798-6670   Fax 626 398-0642

Members Click Here
*for online access
and pricing*

BBB ONLINE
RELIABILITY
PROGRAM
☞ *To become a*
Member Click Here

In the Equifax and Trans Union credit reports you can find a segment called COLLECTIONS, which shows what had been reported to the credit bureau as collection items. The amount owe and the balance remained can also be found. Generally speaking, you don't want to see too many items listed in here.

COLLECTIONS

CREDITOR 1	REPORTED	COLL AMT	STATUS
ID	BAL/PD	COLL BAL	
AG/REMARKS			
HIGHER EDUCATION	4/93 4	1700 6	ADJUSTMENT 8
999X9999 2	5/93 5	1000 7	
SUBJECT DISPUTES THIS ACCOUNT 3			

Signature options

After all the background checking processes, if you finally decide to go ahead and ship the order, be sure to use the shipment tracking option so you can keep track of what is going on with your shipment. Also, always request for a signature on delivery. For higher price item, request for signature with ID verification.

Carrier such as Fedex offers different signature options. For example, its "Indirect Signature Required" option allows delivery when a signature is available from any person at the delivery address; or from a neighbor, building manager or other person at a neighboring address; or the recipient can sign a FedEx door tag authorizing release of the package without anyone present. A slightly better option is the "Direct Signature Required" option, which requires a signature from any person at the delivery address. The best option for expensive item is the "Adult Signature Required" option, which requires a signature from any person at least 21 years old, with government-issued photo identification inspection at the delivery address.

Proof of delivery

The "Proof of Delivery" option is another MUST HAVE option. It allows you to verify receipt of your shipment with delivery signatures (signature tracking that is). Most carriers are now offering to send signature images to you via FTP, CD-ROM, fax or mail, whichever you prefer. Remember, in case of a dispute, you need to submit to your merchant bank the proof of delivery in a timely manner - we are talking about 7 days or less here. So you need to ensure that you always keep a record of every single proof of delivery.

Signature validity

A seasoned chargeback guru can argue around the issue of signature validity. He can claim that the signature collected does not belong to him. However, with such a bold argument he will risk getting the police involved, especially when a photo-ID has been inspected at the time of the delivery. He will have to explain his relationship with the guy who received the item. He will run into further trouble if it is suspected by the police that forged government issued photo ID had been used.

iii There are dangerous things that you should totally avoid. Using UPS as an example, when the customer does not make himself available to receive your shipment when UPS returns for reattempted delivery, he may be entitled to the options of signing the back of the InfoNotice authorizing the driver to leave the package in front of his door. He may also request to have the package delivered to an alternate address.

"I recently sent an item to a home address via recorded delivery after payment has been received. Day 1 delivery attempted but nobody was at home, so a pickup card was left by the postal service reminding the buyer to collect the item from the local sorting office. Day 5 a non-receipt dispute was logged with the credit card company. Day 7 the seller told the buyer to go to the sorting office to retrieve the item but the buyer didn't. Day 15 the buyer went to the sorting office, scribbled a signature on the collection form and took the item. Day 30 an item not received claim was established and chargeback was successful. As the signature held by the postal service was only a scribble, the seller lost both the $ and the item."

When you make your shipment make it explicit that none of these options are to be allowed. Make it an explicit requirement that the item must be delivered to the address you have specified, and that someone must be there to sign for the delivery. Communicate this requirement to your customer at the time the order is placed.

For your information...

When there is solid proof that an item is delivered to the correct address, then even if the purchaser claims that he has never authorized such purchase, he will have to return the item to you (often at his expense), or the police will make sure he does.

Beware of minors

One most commonly encountered type of fraud in the hobby industry is unauthorized purchase made by kids without parental consent. Somehow many parents fail to control access to their credit card or Paypal accts. Even worse, they almost always insist that their kids are innocent.

Since this kind of fraud happens mostly to businesses that have minors as the primary users of the goods being sold, some forms of age verification mechanism may be necessary. For example, in the airsoft industry (airsoft is a form of paintball like replica which shoots plastic bullets), it is not uncommon for retailers to enforce rules like these:

Under no circumstances will XXX sell airsoft to minors. In order to purchase any replica firearm (spring, gas, or electric airsoft gun) from XXX, you must be 18 years of age or older. Before we can complete and ship any order, you must verify by telephone that you are at least 18 years old. If you are under 18, you MUST have your parents' permission, and they must call to verify their age and acknowledge they are your legal guardian.

Some retailers even go extra miles by requiring their customers to fax in a copy of their picture ID which clearly shows birth date information. The benefit of such mechanism is two fold – you verify their age (at least you have done your best to do so, so you are legally safe) and you also verify their identity (thus discouraging potential payment fraud).

Warning: be prepared to lose some businesses – some people would just feel bad faxing in their ID information over a distance.

What if he pays by check?

Set guidelines regarding the types of checks (and money orders) your business will accept. Make sure you let everyone know in advance your check policy. Personal checks in the same state can take up to one week to get cleared. Personal checks from a different state can take even longer to clear.

Clearing foreign checks

Foreign checks (checks issued by a foreign bank) can take 30 to 60 days just to get cleared. As an attempt to protect themselves against fraud, your local banks will almost always impose an additional waiting period on deposits made with foreign checks. The technical term is "balance on hold" – the balance is shown on your statement but is not available for actual use.

ᵢᵢᵢ It is always unsafe to ship before a check is completely cleared.

When a check is received, have it examined very carefully. The extra effort involved in carefully scrutinizing every check will pay off. Surprisingly, most fraudsters are quite careless – they either have an incorrect routing number printed on the check, or the print job is so poor that you can tell the difference right away.

Check verification

The very basic thing to do when verifying a check is to make sure a name, address and phone number are printed on the check. The address printed on the check is going to be the address you'll use for shipping after the check is cleared. **Don't ship to anywhere else.**

You should also pay attention to the feel of the check. Checks printed unprofessionally often have different weight and texture.

Verifying checks...

Forged checks are getting harder and harder to spot. However, you can still recognize some signs of fraudulent checks:

- Checks that don't contain a MICR line. A MICR (Magnetic Ink Character Recognition) line has a specially shaped collection of numbers and symbols for which automated reading equipment was developed years ago in the banking industry. It is seen on the bottom of all U.S. and Canadian Checks, eCommerce Drafts, and deposit slip printing.
- Checks that lack perforations. All legitimate checks are perforated on

at least one edge.

- Toner pile-up on the check, which is a sign of a check generated on a color copier or an inkjet printer.
- Misspelled pre-printed words on the check.
- An incorrect Federal Reserve District number in the routing number. The number should match the location of the institution on which the check is drawn. If you are not in the banking industry you may have difficulties identifying the routing number. However, a call to the issuing bank may help you clear up the picture.

The four-digits following the MICR number at the bottom of the check should always match the four-digit number at the top right hand of the check. Also, all checks (except government checks) should have a perforation along one side of the check. We like to recommend that you refer to the two sources listed below for further information on the various check elements:

http://www.sxlist.com/techref/ecommerce/routeno/index.htm

http://www.checkcomposer.com/Downloads/CheckFraud.pdf

Forged check

Note that even though you may compare the signature on the check with that on the identification a customer provided, both of them can be forged – there is no point on comparing a forged signature with a forged identification. The best thing you can do is to directly verify the check through its issuing bank (some banks will perform this service for depositors while some will not).

For your reference, in most states and foreign countries it is a felony for someone to write a check knowing that it will not be honored by the bank:

"A person who commits the offense of deposit account fraud by the making, drawing, uttering, executing, or delivering of an instrument on a bank of another state shall be guilty of a felony and, upon conviction thereof, shall be punished by imprisonment for not less than one nor more than XXX years or by a fine in an amount of up to $XXXXX, or both."

Proving the crime is often not easy though ☹

➡ **As an advice ...**

Make sure you never accept second-party or third-party checks. A fraudster may tell you that it is way too difficult and complicated to send you the money directly from his state or country, so he'll arrange for someone in your state to send you a check. Say NO to this. You should insist on shipping only to where the check came from.

Check bouncing

Apart from using a forged check, a fraudster may use a valid check that is not backed by sufficient fund in the bank. Keep in mind, most returned checks have low check numbers (i.e. check number in the range of 100 to 500). In fact, low check numbers indicate a recently opened account, which is a potentially risky source of check.

For your information...

Even when a check is cleared, you may still have trouble if the check is later on found to be problematic. Under federal law, banks have to do their best to make funds available to you ASAP – usually within five business days. But just because you can withdraw the money doesn't mean the check is good (even if it's a cashier's check). Sometimes it may take weeks or months for a forgery to be discovered and the corresponding check to bounce. When a check bounces, your bank will deduct the amount that was originally credited to your account. If there isn't enough to cover the loss, the bank will attempt to take money from other accounts you have over there, or even sue you for damage.

Check by fax

There are certain software solutions out there which can allow a merchant to take check information from the customer (by email/phone/fax) and then print a check for deposit. What is risky about this process is that the customer may later claim that those information supplied at a distance is actually stolen information. And since the customer's signature is absent on the check you print, rebuttal could be very easy.

Other alternatives: COD, LC and Escrow

Your customers would always want to protect themselves by not paying with some seemingly risky methods. As said by a user on an internet forum, "The fraudsters of the world prefer Western Union, TT and PayPal payments..." So you know that Western Union and Bank Transfer are quite unwelcome for making payments.

For your information...
With Western Union or bank TT there is virtually no way for the buyer to get his money back should fraud occur. This is why most buyers are reluctant to pay via these methods.

A seemingly fairer way to pay is through COD (Cash On Delivery). With it, payment for goods would be made at the time of delivery. If the purchaser refuses to pay while the goods are delivered, the goods will be returned back to the seller. The seller would still have to bear the cost of shipment (both ways) plus the processing fee involved, but risks can be minimized without frustrating the buyer too much (and without costing you too much for using the service – UPS, Fedex and most other carriers are happy to make COD arrangement for you with a small fee).

For your information...

Some people dislike COD because it doesn't give them a chance to inspect the good prior to making payment.

If the purchase carries a very high dollar value (talking about thousands of dollars here) and the transaction is cross border, you may want to consider accepting LC (Letter Of Credit). A LC is basically a letter from a bank guaranteeing that payment to a seller will be received after the bank receives confirmation that the goods have been properly delivered. This is an ideal arrangement that can protect both sides. HOWEVER, using LC is not cheap at all as the banks involved (both your bank and your customer's bank) would charge a service fee (often no less than hundreds of dollars). Therefore you should use it only if the goods in question are of real high value, that the cost of the LC can be fully justified.

For your information...

Not all banks provide LC related services, so you must check with yours and see what they can do for you.

Escrow services such as http://www.safefunds.com/ may also be used if trust is lacking between the trading parties. Instead of sending money or goods directly to each other, the escrow service would withhold the money first until the goods are formally accepted by the buyer. Escrow services are generally less costly than LC, and that they can be used even for short distance trading. However, there are bogus escrow services out there that could put you into big troubles. Therefore, do your research and choose a reputable one before making any commitment.

For your information...

Most escrow services would allow thorough inspection of the goods prior to releasing payment.

Against the "item not as described" claim and

the "item damaged" claim

You may wonder: "The measures mentioned so far don't really protect me against the item not as described / item damaged claim?"

True. In fact, there can be so many variations of the "item not as described/item damaged" fraud, which makes it very difficult for a merchant to stay completely safe. However, his bank doesn't like to receive too many chargeback requests from him either. By repeatedly using the item not as described/item damaged trick he is making himself more suspicious than necessary.

<u>You can actually give yourself more protection by:</u>

✓ Stating clearly your "warranty period". For example, you guarantee your product against defect for a period of 30 days counting from the day the item is received, that any claim must be made within this period directly to you, NOT through the bank. FYI, the longer the customer keeps the item, the more difficult it would be for him to use the "item not as described/item damaged" trick as he is expected to raise the issue up within a reasonable time frame.

Keeping records of all documentations, including product descriptions, pictures of the goods shipped (with date shown on the pictures), shipping receipt …etc. You need to have all these documents handy when a dispute arises.

Insist on buying shipping insurance against loss and damage of shipment, so if something extremely problematic happens you can still get the carrier involved in the investigation. One typical trick used by the chargeback gurus involves claiming that the item arrived is damaged on arrival when in fact it was himself who abused and damaged the item. By having insurance coverage on the shipment he has the obligation to submit proof of damage to the carrier. If he refuses to submit such proof then you may use it as a legitimate defense against his claim. To make this approach as effective as possible, you may want to spell out clearly in your business policy that it is his obligation to show proof of damage to the carrier in a timely manner should claim for damage arise, or he is effectively giving up his rights on such claim. Have him sign on a hard copy of your business policy when the order is placed to show that he had noted and agreed to abide by your rules. **Do this for expensive items. The extra workload involved would be justified.**

Be sure to make it clear that he must retain all packaging material, boxes and bags ...etc when filing a damaged item claim. You want to do this because this is how you can identify potential fraud. When you ship your box, your carrier must have measured the weight of the entire package, including all packaging material of course. By finding out any significant discrepancy in weight between the original package and the returned package you can tell whether fraud has taken place. Let's say if the customer wants to accuse you of shipping him a box of stones, he must assemble a package of stones which gives the same weight, or he is effectively telling you that he is lying.

So would it be safer through item pick-up in person?

No, not always. In fact, whenever someone come and pick up the item, always follow these guidelines:

✓ Always have him come in person, along with his picture ID (such as his driver license). Make it clear beforehand that he must come in person, not by his girl friend nor his brother.

✓ At the time he shows up, check his picture ID for verification. Make sure the name on his ID matches exactly the name on his credit card. Compare the signature, photo and physical description of the ID with that of the check writer. If he is showing you his driver's license, make sure it is smooth all over with no ridges that indicate an alteration or modification. And most importantly, check the "Valid until" section - verify that the ID is still valid.

For your information...

Most adult picture IDs include some unalterable physical descriptions of the corresponding person (hair color as an example).

✔ Ask him to sign a release form to acknowledge the pickup.

✔ Always remember to record the license plate number of his vehicle. You don't have to do it right in front of him, but do it. This provides a much easier way for the police to track him down if necessary.

✔ Don't accept any form of check payment on the spot. You won't be able to guarantee the availability and legality of funds in such a short time frame. You would have to either charge his credit card beforehand, or accept cash on the spot. OR, insist on a cashiers check for the exact amount from a bank that has a branch in your area so you can perform an instant verification.

iii One major mistake people make is to believe in the excuses made up by the fraudsters. Something like "I couldn't have time to visit the bank and I forgot to bring my ATM card with me. Can I write you a check please as I really need the item now..."; "Sorry for such a short notice but I really need to use the item tomorrow morning so can I come and pick it up right now and settle payment through a money order?" ... **Remember, regardless of how sincere they appear to be, don't allow for any exceptions. Always strictly adhere to the above guidelines.**

→ **As an advice ...**
Have yourself alerted if he is buying several thousand dollars worth of goods but is driving a 20-year old dirt cheap vehicle. Could he really afford the purchase?

Justifying the extra workloads

Now you may question if it really is worth the time and effort spent on investigating a customer to such extent. Well, there are always tradeoffs, and you need to balance the extra workloads against the risks. Again, if the likelihood of getting defrauded is high and the loss may be substantial, then you should do it.

Before you go the extra miles, however, there are some early signs of fraudulent attempts (mostly in the form of unauthorized payment claim) that can get you alerted:

✓ They insist on using email addresses provided by free services such as yahoo and gmail (where identity check is almost totally absent) for communication. The email addresses typically do not resemble the names of the users but some random combinations of words and phrases and numbers. For example, something like hkpro21@yahoo.com, pinoboy@gmail.com ...etc.

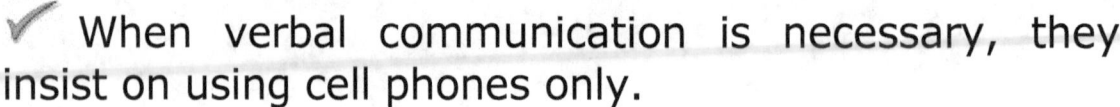 When verbal communication is necessary, they insist on using cell phones only.

✓ They refuse to come over and pick up the goods in person even if they live pretty close to your location.

✓ They ask you to rush shipments and are willing to pay extra high S/H for overnight delivery.

Personally, I would accept a big ticket order for overnight delivery only if payment is made in advance by cash (so you can have time to verify the cash notes received!!!).

Call for help from the police force

Regardless of how careful you are, there may still be a chance for you to miss one or two fraudulent intents. If unfortunately you run into unexpected trouble, the key to weather through it is to act fast. Don't delay. Have all your documentations handy, and call up the police department of the fraudster's home town (i.e. the police department closest to the delivery address).

To ensure that the police will entertain your request, have all the necessary proof ready as hard copies:

✓ All email conversations between you and the fraudster.

✓ Payment confirmation (credit card receipt, bank deposit slip ...etc)

✓ Product description and pictures.

✓ Full tracking report and delivery confirmation.

✓ Name, address and phone number of the fraudster. It is vital for this address to be the same as the delivery address, as the delivery address is where the fraud has occurred.

✓ A copy of the written correspondence sent by the bank informing you of the fraudulent transaction.

⋮⋮⋮ Make your message to the police very clear:

"A guy named [the customer name] from [the shipping address] used a stolen card to purchase $xxx worth of goods from us. We have been informed by the card issuer that the transaction is fraudulent."

If the police are willing to act fast per your request, it is quite likely that some of the lost items can be recovered (unless the fraudster has moved overnight). Be sure to emphasize to the police that this is actually a criminal offense, not simply a business transaction dispute. Police officers would act only if the case has sufficient criminal element(s) in it.

You can easily find out the phone number and other contact information of the local police department through doing a simple search on Yahoo or Google. For example, in the search field just type in "san jose" "police department", then you will be able to retrieve the web address of the SJPD:

End of book

Comments and questions may be sent to:

editor@antifraudbible.com

For further information on our publications please visit:

www.antifraudbible.com

www.ingramcontent.com/pod-product-compliance
Lightning Source LLC
Chambersburg PA
CBHW081138170526
45165CB00008B/2719